BRAVELY

"The very least you can do in your life is to figure out what you hope for. The most you can do is live inside that hope, running down its hallways, touching the walls on both sides."

BARBARA KINGSOLVER
WRITER

•

"The size of your dreams must always exceed your current capacity to achieve them. If your dreams do not scare you, they are not big enough."

ELLEN JOHNSON SIRLEAF
PRESIDENT OF LIBERIA

•

"Life itself is the proper binge."

JULIA CHILD
CHEF

Bravely Journal

A GUIDED JOURNAL FOR IMAGINING A FUTURE YOU'LL LOVE

RP STUDIO

PHILADELPHIA

What's inside . . .

Yours and yours alone.

This guided journal is designed to help you imagine the future beyond.

No rules.

If you yearn for structure as you take on the world, then capture your thoughts one day at a time. Perhaps dip in and dip out at pivotal moments. Or jot down a thought when you've had an aha. As you carve out "me time" in a favorite place, mindfully gather what moves you and dwell on the "why." You may discover that the process of journaling moves you forward as you take on a rocky or uncharted path.

Creativity unleashed.

Within these pages are tools to aid your journaling and journey. When you crave space to capture what's on your mind, put pen or pencil or even crayon to the blank pages. Add a bullet list or sketch . . . whatever you wish. If a nudge is what's needed, then draft your own thoughts off of the quotations . . . wise words drawn from real-life experiences of some of the world's greats. You'll find cues, thought starters, list builders, and timelines designed to get you unstuck while you chronicle meaningful moments and traditions you hold dear. In the back, you'll discover pithy bios of each quoteur complete with related books, podcasts, videos, sites, and such for when you feel the urge to dig deeper into their insights or be inspired by someone else's story.

Revisit your story.

Choose a date: your birthday, the last day (or first) of each year, an anniversary or milestone that's important to you. Then look back on where you've been. Reflecting on what helps make you *you* is powerful fuel for your dreams as you work to accomplish goals big and small.

So drift through the pages. Linger on words. Get riled up. Cherish what's nostalgic. Celebrate successes. Note happenstances. Record trip-ups as well. Dwell on who and what inspire you to be your best you. Maybe share here and there.

By giving voice to your own ideas, experiences, and beliefs, your story will become clear—with all of its glorious, messy layers—and help you bravely shape a bold, creative, compassionate future you'll love.

CHEERS!
PAULINE & ALICIA

Each of us has a story to tell.

•

Tell yours.

•

To yourself.
(Then, perhaps, to the world.)

About you.

Your birth name

Who you're named after

The name you go by

Nicknames that have stuck

Nicknames that have been retired (those endearing ones that conjure up memories)

Where you grew up

You call this your hometown

You call this home

The loves of your life . . . family and friends

Big idea.

Date

_____

My "someday" dream . . .

"Dream big and dream fierce."

VIOLA DAVIS
ACTOR

Free space . . .

For gathering all sorts of things you don't want to forget from your journey so far.

"It's really important to appreciate the moment that you're in."

NICOLE STOTT

SPACEWALKER

"I can't tell you how to succeed, but I can tell you how to fail:
Try to please everyone."

ELEANOR ROOSEVELT

FIRST LADY

·

"Yes, it's true I'm here, and I'm just as strange as you."

FRIDA KAHLO

PAINTER

·

"I'm going to do what I want to do. I'm going to be who I really am.
I'm going to figure out what that is."

EMMA WATSON

ACTOR

AUTHENTICALLY

"

Let go of who you think
you're supposed to be and
embrace who you are.

"

BRENÉ BROWN
SOCIAL WORKER

Let it go.

We've all felt it—the social pressure to put on an act, to pose, to try to be something other than who we are. Below, write down any expectations that you've felt bound to conform to . . .

AT HOME & AT WORK • IN RELATIONSHIPS & SOCIAL SETTINGS • WITHIN COMMUNITIES & OUT IN THE WIDER WORLD

Come back to this page when you need a reminder to drop the pose and live your truth.

66

To respect tradition is the best
way to innovate without ever losing
your identity.

99

NICOLETTA SPAGNOLI
FASHION CEO • CANDYMAKER

Your take.

•

Nicoletta Spagnoli has a sweet heritage. Her great grandmother, renowned Italian fashion designer Luisa Spagnoli, invented Baci Perugina chocolates, wrapping each "kiss" with a love note. For a century, the family has kept the original idea fresh by mixing in humor, puzzles, multiple languages, pop lyrics, and even custom messages. We might not all hail from a fashion and confectionery dynasty, but we all have identities shaped by our backgrounds, traditions, and past experiences. Respecting these parts of ourselves can be a genuine source of strength and distinctiveness as we map our futures.

•

What traditions and legacies are important to you moving forward? Freely list them below.

"

You gotta put yourself out there.
And in order to put yourself out there,
you've gotta have an idea
of who you are.

"

TIFFANY HADDISH
COMEDIAN

Her story. Your story.

You can bring your whole self to your work. Being your genuine self can also bring people to your work.

•

Stand-up comedian Tiffany Haddish has a rep for disarming authenticity. Dishing up truth bombs and not being afraid to admit when she's a "hot mess" are what make her act hilarious. Her candidness—about how she first turned to comedy to cope with a bumpy childhood, including a tough stint in foster care, and about how difficult it was to make it in the industry—is equally inspiring. Today, the breakout movie star still counts "seeing teeth" when audiences laugh out loud as her greatest joy, which always makes her wonder—should she have been a dentist instead?

•

What makes you uniquely you? How can you put yourself out there?

When have you felt most empowered to "do you"?

Being authentic can be personally fulfilling. It can also change the world around you.

·

How could you use your differences to make a difference?

"When you don't dress like everyone else, you don't have to
think like everyone else."

IRIS APFEL
INTERIOR DESIGNER TURNED LATE-BREAKING FASHION ICON

"Being different is a superpower."

GRETA THUNBERG

TEEN CLIMATE CHANGE CRUSADER WHO'S
ACTIVATED A GLOBAL KID-LED MOVEMENT

Timeline

Fill this timeline in for past revelations or record your insights in real time. Appreciate those moments when your true self suddenly shines through or take note of experiences that taught you something about yourself!

The real me moment:

_____

What it revealed:

_____

_____

_____

_____

Date: ....

The real me moment:

_____

What it revealed:

_____

_____

_____

_____

Date: ....

The real me moment:

_____

What it revealed:

_____

_____

_____

_____

Date: ....

The real me moment:

_____

What it revealed:

_____

_____

_____

_____

Date: ....

The real me moment:

_____

What it revealed:

_____

_____

_____

_____

Date: ....

The real me moment:

_____

What it revealed:

_____

_____

_____

_____

Date: ....

"Everything you want to be, you already are.
You're simply on the path to discovering it."

ALICIA KEYS
CLASSICALLY TRAINED PIANIST • SINGER-SONGWRITER •
15-TIME GRAMMY WINNER

"

Decide first what is authentic,
then go after it with all your heart.

"

LOUISE ERDRICH
AUTHOR

Words to live by.

Here's space to write down your own personal affirmation,
a quote that reminds you to be yourself—could be your words,
could be someone else's . . .

"To me, the only sin is mediocrity."

MARTHA GRAHAM

MOTHER OF MODERN DANCE

•

"I find the lure of the unknown irresistible."

SYLVIA EARLE

AQUANAUT

•

"If there's one thing I'm willing to bet on, it's myself."

BEYONCÉ

POP ICON

BOLDLY

66

Be that risk-taker and leader in your own life. The first person you have to convince about anything is yourself.

99

SYLVIA ACEVEDO

ENGINEER

Your take on risk-taking.

•

Sylvia Acevedo's daring career trajectory has included titles from rocket scientist to startup founder to education reformer. Now, as a professional emboldener of the next gen of go-getters, she's a model and advocate for taking "smart" risks in order to grow.

•

How do you decide whether a risk's worth taking? Where do you personally draw the line on what you're willing to put on the line?

Peek at this page when you're weighing your next big move.

take a hiatus to delve deeply into your beliefs

commit to attempting a physical feat

ACT WITHOUT WAITING FOR PERMISSION

BRING YOUR OWN CHAIR TO THE TABLE OF DECISION-MAKERS

plant your own fruit & veg, maybe sell them in town

REACH OUT TO SOMEONE YOU ASPIRE TO BE LIKE

compose a song, write your memoir, learn the cha-cha

TAKE A DEEP DIVE INTO A TOPIC CLOSE TO YOUR HEART & SHARE YOUR RESEARCH

GET SAVVY ABOUT THE STOCK MARKET AND YOUR PERSONAL TOLERANCE FOR RISK

say "yes" to a public speaking opportunity

LEARN TO CODE & CREATE A TECH SOLUTION TO A PROBLEM THAT'S BEEN NAGGING YOU

SCOUT OUT A COLLABORATOR FROM BEYOND YOUR NORMAL SPACE TO GROW SOMETHING NEW

BECOME GOOD AT SOMETHING, THEN TEACH SOMEONE ELSE

STRAY OFF THE BEATEN PATH & FIND YOURSELF A NEW SET OF LOCALS

post a video that might just go viral

run for local office

Embracing that beginner's mindset.

•

Among these acts are real-world examples of turning-point moments for the remarkable women quoted in this journal. Unfamiliarity can often set off our own internal alarm bells, signaling danger when we venture into new domains. But some friction can be a good thing. Challenge yourself to take healthy risks because they may evolve into something grand. Look for those things that actually rev up your brain and keep you from becoming comfortable or complacent. Find those things that, for you, are not business as usual. Stretch into the unmapped, and you might just find a hidden path to your purpose.

•

Now it's your turn to be adventurous.
Tee up smart risks—mini or major—you could take in your life.

"

Don't change yourself; change the game.

"

HALIMA ADEN

MODEL

Her story. Your story.

**Sometimes just being yourself or standing up for
your values can be a bold move.**

•

When Halima Aden became the first ever contestant to wear a hijab and burkini
during the Miss Minnesota USA beauty pageant, she took a step outside her
"comfort zone." That small but decisive step turned out to be the first in a game-
changing journey that has seen the Somali refugee emerge as high fashion's
inaugural hijab-wearing top model. Besides inspiring a new market for modest-
chic looks, Halima has been able to use the catwalk to become a cover girl for
education, mental health, and humanitarian aid.

•

**Describe one or more moments when you decided to take a step
(or leap!) outside of your comfort zone.**

Halima's bold move led to unexpected transformations in the fashion industry and society.

•

If you could spark a revolution, what would it be?

"What would you attempt to do if you knew you could not fail?"

REGINA DUGAN

INVENTOR & TECH EXEC WHO BECAME THE FIRST
FEMALE HEAD OF US DEFENSE RESEARCH

"It's about an evolution, not a revolution—
but I'll always try for revolutions."

VERA WANG

FASHION EDITOR WHOSE FIRST FORAY INTO DESIGN
FOREVER CHANGED THE BRIDAL INDUSTRY

Timeline

Keep track of moments from this point forward when you've had an audacious aha, committed to a bold course of action, or made a move—big or small—that expanded your personal horizons.

Big move or bold idea:

_____

_____

_____

_____

_____

_____

Date: ....

Big move or bold idea:

_____

_____

_____

_____

_____

_____

Date: ....

Big move or bold idea:

_____

_____

_____

_____

_____

_____

Date: ....

Big move or bold idea:

_____

_____

_____

_____

_____

Date: ....

Big move or bold idea:

_____

_____

_____

_____

_____

Date: ....

Big move or bold idea:

_____

_____

_____

_____

_____

_____

Date: ....

"You need big moves. If you're going to dance, you gotta really dance."

STEVIE NICKS
WOULD-BE BALLERINA • SINGER-SONGWRITER •
MESMERIZING PERFORMER

66

The world is in perpetual motion and
we must invent the things of tomorrow.
One must go before others, be
determined and exacting, and let
your intelligence guide your life.
Act with audacity.

99

MADAME CLICQUOT
GRANDE DAME OF CHAMPAGNE

Words to live by.

Pop. Clink. Fizz. Script a toast to your own audacity or log a quote that puts you in a carpe diem mindset!

"One's feelings waste themselves in words; they ought all to be distilled into actions, and into actions which bring results."

FLORENCE NIGHTINGALE
FOUNDER OF MODERN NURSING

·

"Knowing what must be done does away with fear."

ROSA PARKS
CIVIL RIGHTS ICON

·

"Life is not so much what you accomplish
as what you overcome."

ROBIN ROBERTS
BROADCASTER

BRAVELY

"

I'm stronger than fear.

"

MALALA YOUSAFZAI
EDUCATION ACTIVIST • SURVIVOR

Own it.

Being afraid isn't a bad thing. It certainly alerts you to dangers. But it can also teach you what you care about and be a positive sign that you're pushing yourself. What scares you? Put your fears into words.

SUSPICIONS & PHOBIAS • DOUBTS & UNCERTAINTIES • PERSONAL WORRIES & PUBLIC CONCERNS

Bravery doesn't mean living without fear. It's all in how you face it.

"

You can't do it alone . . .
Find a group of people who
challenge and inspire you.
Spend a lot of time with them,
and it will change your life.

"

AMY POEHLER
COMEDIAN • ACTOR • PRODUCER

Your role models, muses & heroes.

We all stand on the shoulders of those brave folks who've come before and find strength from their inspiring lives and work.
Take this opportunity to assemble your crew of heartening role models, both ones you know personally and ones you admire from afar.

I want to . . .

Believe like

Build like

Care like

Create like

Dare like

Dream like

Experiment like

Give like

Imagine like

Innovate like

Inspire like

Lead like

Live like

Perform like

Persevere like

Stand up like

Speak out like

> We are the builders. And so we build, even amid chaos and disintegration. . . . We build and we build, shift after shift, as fast—and as best—as we can.

SIMONE HANNAH-CLARK
ICU NURSE

> This is not the day I'm going to give up.

SARAH ROSENAL
CARDIOLOGIST

Her story. Your story.

•

When we cultivate bravery, it helps us cope with those trials we could never have predicted. Every gnarly twist in the road is an opportunity to grow courage. These quotes are from two women working on the front lines of the coronavirus crisis—an Aussie intensive care nurse who helped deal with the Brooklyn outbreak and a cardiology fellow with three young children who volunteered to interrupt her training to serve in her hospital's COVID-19 unit.

The global pandemic introduced levels of fear, uncertainty, sacrifice, and disruption that people seldom encounter in a lifetime. In the face of monumental challenges, we found ourselves surrounded by everyday heroes—health care workers and teachers, cashiers and cleaners, transit operators and delivery drivers, small business owners and essential manufacturers—who refused to give up. Others stayed home, spread hope, found solutions, and used the slowdown to press reset. Many dealt with unimaginable losses.

Each of us summoned courage that strengthened who we are and shaped what we—and our world—are becoming.

•

Describe how you met this or another unexpected challenge in your life. What, in the chaos, helped you get through?

What tough lessons, coping strategies, and hopeful examples did you take away from this experience to help you meet the next occasion for bravery?

"When things are as bad as ever they can be, you cease to mind them much. You set your teeth and battle with the fates."

GERTRUDE BELL
EXPLORER-ARCHAEOLOGIST TURNED INFLUENTIAL
BRITISH POLITICAL ADVISER IN THE MIDDLE EAST

"What a crazy, unsolicited adventure all of this is."

SIMONE GIERTZ

MILLENNIAL INVENTOR & FAN-FAVORITE ROBOT ENTHUSIAST

WHO'S BATTLING A BRAIN TUMOR

Timeline

We aren't born brave. It takes practice.
Use this timeline to record the everyday acts of courage you carry out.
Before you know it, "couraging" will be a habit.

Small victory:

_____

_____

_____

_____

_____

Date: ....

Small victory:

_____

_____

_____

_____

_____

Date: ....

Small victory:

_____

_____

_____

_____

_____

Date: ....

Small victory:

_____

_____

_____

_____

_____

Date: ....

Small victory:

_____

_____

_____

_____

_____

Date: ....

Small victory:

_____

_____

_____

_____

_____

_____

Date: ....

"Courage is a habit, a virtue: You get it by courageous acts. It's like you learn to swim by swimming. You learn courage by couraging."

MARY DALY
PHILOSOPHER • RADICAL THEOLOGIAN • TEACHER

*Your bravest self
will be your best self.*

MELLODY HOBSON
INVESTOR • BOARD CHAIR

Words to live by.

Here's space to ink a motto that stirs the everyday hero in you.

"The fruit of love is service, which is compassion in action."

MOTHER TERESA
SAINT

•

"I really don't know why I care so much. I just have something inside me that tells me that there is a problem, and I have got to do something about it. . . . I'm sure it's the same voice that is speaking to everybody on this planet."

WANGARI MAATHAI
NOBEL PEACE PRIZE LAUREATE

•

"Whatever suffering we see, no matter how bad it is, we can help if we don't lose hope and we don't turn away."

MELINDA GATES
PHILANTHROPIST

COMPASSIONATELY

> "Tuning into yourself is the first step toward tuning into others."

SHARON SALZBERG
MEDITATION TEACHER

> "If we are willing to stand fully in our own shoes and never give up on ourselves, then we will be able to put ourselves in the shoes of others and never give up on them. True compassion does not come from wanting to help out those less fortunate than ourselves but from realizing our kinship with all beings."

PEMA CHÖDRÖN
BUDDHIST NUN

Being kind to yourself:

We cannot take care of others if we don't take care of ourselves.
List ways that you practice self-care or could be more
compassionate with yourself . . .

LOOKING AFTER YOUR HEALTH & PROTECTING YOUR
MENTAL WELL-BEING • MINDFULLY PREPPING FOR THE DAY &
RESTING AT NIGHT • BEING COMFORTABLE IN YOUR OWN SHOES
& FORGIVING ANY MISSTEPS • TAKING "YOU" TIME & MAKING SPACE
FOR THE THINGS THAT GIVE YOU WARM FUZZIES

"

My parents' incredible compassion showed me firsthand how to build a better world, one action at a time.

"

CLAIRE BABINEAUX-FONTENOT
FEEDING AMERICA CEO

Paying it forward.

•

Claire Babineaux-Fontenot is the head of the US's largest hunger relief nonprofit with a network of 200 food banks and 16,000 food pantries. She's also one of 108 siblings raised by parents who were heralded for being lifelong foster caregivers and giving all they could in spite of humble circumstances. A cancer diagnosis spurred Claire to reconsider her career as a high-flying business exec and find a new vocation inspired by her parents' lead. Today, she's building a better world by coordinating millions of generous acts to ensure no one goes hungry.

•

Who have been models of compassion for you, either in their actions toward you or on behalf of others?

Note to self: write a letter of gratitude to the people named.

Claire identified her upbringing and confrontation with cancer as life events that moved her to take compassionate action.

•

What personal experiences have made you more empathetic?

"The burdens braved by humankind / Are also the moments
that make us humans kind."

AMANDA GORMAN
STUDENT AUTHOR-ACTIVIST WHO BECAME
THE US'S FIRST YOUTH POET LAUREATE

"

What if we measured true success not by the amount of money you have but by the amount of human energy you unlock, the amount of potential you enable? If that were our metric, our world would be a different place.

"

JACQUELINE NOVOGRATZ
SOCIAL ENTREPRENEUR

Her story. Your story.

•

Jacqueline Novogratz was crunching numbers as an international credit analyst on Wall Street when she decided to unleash a moral revolution in business. She started by coining a new kind of banking based on investing in those at the bottom of the pyramid . . . the bakers and builders, growers and healers who'd otherwise miss out on capital or aid. Her NGO Acumen has provided $110 million and counting to back social enterprises with huge returns: empowering millions of people to better their own lives.

•

How do you measure success in your personal and professional lives?

Jacqueline measures her investments according to the number of people they empower.

•

How does compassion factor into how you gauge your efforts?

"Emotion without action is irrelevant."

JODY WILLIAMS

AID WORKER & NOBEL LAUREATE BEHIND THE
INTERNATIONAL TREATY TO BAN LAND MINES

"I refuse to believe you cannot be both
compassionate and strong."

JACINDA ARDERN
NEW ZEALAND PRIME MINISTER WHO HAS
BECOME AN ICON OF EMPATHETIC LEADERSHIP

Timeline

Fill this in for past revelations or record them in real time.
Acknowledge moments when you've been shown compassion, and
make note of instances when you've given back in big or small ways.

I received:
_____
_____
_____
_____
_____
_____
Date: ....

I gave:
_____
_____
_____
_____
_____
_____
Date: ....

I received:
_____
_____
_____
_____
_____
_____
Date: ....

I gave:

_____

_____

_____

_____

_____

_____

Date: ....

I received:

_____

_____

_____

_____

_____

_____

Date: ....

I gave:

_____

_____

_____

_____

_____

_____

Date: ....

"The open hand is blessed, for it gives in abundance even as it receives."

BIDDY MASON
MIDWIFE • REAL ESTATE ENTREPRENEUR •
FORMER SLAVE TURNED PHILANTHROPIST

"

The most beautiful people we have known are those who have known defeat, known suffering, known struggle, known loss, and have found their way out of the depths. These persons have an appreciation, a sensitivity, and an understanding of life that fills them with compassion, gentleness, and deep loving concern. Beautiful people do not just happen.

"

ELISABETH KÜBLER-ROSS
PSYCHIATRIST

Words to live by.

There are moments in life when we're at a loss for what to say. What words do you call upon in those toughest of times to let someone know you care?

Note down a quotation or message below . . .

"Pretending is not just play. Pretending is imagined possibility."

MERYL STREEP
ACTOR

•

"I'd like to open a door to a world that has yet to be invented."

ZAHA HADID
ARCHITECT

•

"Create whatever causes a revolution in your heart."

ELIZABETH GILBERT
MEMOIRIST

CREATIVELY

> We need to give ourselves time and space for play, space in which the unpredictable can happen.

JULIET KINCHIN

MOMA CURATOR

Your "play list."

Playing isn't simply about relaxing, recharging, and goofing around. It's also the way we learn, unlock our creativity, and make imaginative leaps.
Here are thought starters, mood enhancers, and reminders of good old-fashioned fun to open space for the unpredictable . . .

What leaves me awestruck

What sparks my imagination

What makes me belly-laugh

The most fun I've ever had

The most spontaneous I've ever been

The most serendipitous thing I've ever experienced

My can't-put-down books

My can't-turn-off shows & podcasts

My can't-stop-thinking-about films & art

My favorite mood-setting songs

My favorite ways to express myself

My favorite "playmates"

"Creativity lives in paradox: serious art is born
from serious play."

JULIA CAMERON

ARTIST-AUTHOR-FILMMAKER-COMPOSER FAMOUS
FOR INSPIRING OTHER CREATIVES

How I like to get my hands dirty

How I like to kick off my shoes

How I like to relive my childhood favorites

The places that feed my spirit

The travels that have changed my perspective

The quest or adventures I yearn to take

"You cannot do some of these things and
keep your hair all nice."

MAE JEMISON

DANCER TURNED PEACE CORPS DOCTOR TURNED
TRAILBLAZING ASTRONAUT TURNED TECH FOUNDER

> " "

I like crossing the imaginary
boundaries we set up between different
fields—it's very refreshing.

" "

MARYAM MIRZAKHANI

MATHEMATICIAN

Her story. Your story.

•

Maryam Mirzakhani spent her childhood in Iran dreaming of being a novelist.
So when math kindled her creative spirit, she ended up approaching tough
calculations like stories whose characters would evolve toward an ending she
couldn't predict. The late Stanford prof's inventive use of tools and theories that
had never been mixed before helped her solve problems that had long been
considered unsolvable, and helped her make history as the first woman to
win mathematics' highest prize, the Fields Medal.

•

Describe a time when you solved a problem in a creative or unusual way.

How might you look outside of your field or beyond your current toolbox to find an unconventional solution to a problem you're facing?

"Creativity is a lot like looking at the world through a kaleidoscope. You look at a set of elements, the same ones everyone else sees, but then reassemble those floating bits and pieces into an enticing new possibility."

ROSABETH MOSS KANTER

SOCIAL SCIENTIST TURNED LEADING BUSINESS
PROF & INNOVATION EXPERT

"You don't have to shout to get someone's attention."

LOUISE FILI

VINTAGE-INSPIRED TYPOGRAPHER TURNED
LEGENDARY DESIGN STUDIO FOUNDER

Creativity doesn't require a divine muse. Humans are naturally creative, and our inventiveness can be ignited by the simplest things or chance encounters in our daily lives.
Use this timeline to trace some unexpected catalysts that spark your imagination.

Everyday inspiration:

_____

What it kindled:

_____

_____

_____

_____

Date: ....

Everyday inspiration:

_____

What it kindled:

_____

_____

_____

_____

Date: ....

Everyday inspiration:

_____

What it kindled:

_____

_____

_____

_____

Date: ....

Everyday inspiration:

_____

What it kindled:

_____

_____

_____

_____

Date: ....

Everyday inspiration:

_____

What it kindled:

_____

_____

_____

_____

Date: ....

Everyday inspiration:

_____

What it kindled:

_____

_____

_____

_____

Date: ....

"Everything is inspiration when you're looking at the world.
Everything I do in life, everything I touch, is something that I embrace,
that I cherish, and something that I care about."

DOMINIQUE CRENN
"REBEL CHEF" • FOOD ACTIVIST • 3-TIME MICHELIN STAR WINNER

"
You can't use up creativity.
The more you use, the more you have.

"

MAYA ANGELOU
AUTHOR • HUMANITARIAN

Words to live by.

Here's space to capture a quote from a muse of yours—someone whose ideas or story you find thrillingly creative.

"Like what you do, and then you will do your best."

KATHERINE JOHNSON
NASA MATHEMATICIAN

•

"If I had to nominate a driving force in my life,
I'd plump for passion every time."

ANITA RODDICK
SOCIAL ENTREPRENEUR

•

"Pursue your passion, and everything else will fall into place.
This is not being romantic. This is the highest order of pragmatism."

GABBY GIFFORDS
ADVOCATE

PASSIONATELY

"

What really inspires me is seeing what someone is willing to sacrifice for, what they care about in this life, because through that you can see what someone loves.

"

SARAH LEWIS
ART HISTORIAN

Your loves.

•

When we truly love something, we're often prepared to put our time, resources, stamina, reputations, and even livelihoods on the line for it.

•

What have you sacrificed for? What are you willing to sacrifice for? Answering those questions is one way to figure out what you're deeply passionate about. Freely list your responses below.

WHAT OR WHO . . . MOTIVATES YOU? • ANIMATES YOU? •
GETS YOU OUT OF BED IN THE MORNING?

66

Enthusiasm is my superpower.
One might say that confidence yields
the same result. I disagree.
Confidence is about yourself,
enthusiasm is about something
else. Confidence is impressive, but
enthusiasm is infectious. Confidence
is serious, enthusiasm is fun.

99

TINA ROTH EISENBERG
DESIGNER

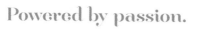

Powered by passion.

•

Swiss-born designer Tina Roth Eisenberg is a serial entrepreneur who's founded everything from a temporary tattoo company to a coworking studio. The morning lecture series she launched—CreativeMornings—quickly turned into an international movement taken up in nearly 200 cities, proving just how smart, in tune, infectious, and fun Tina's enthusiasm can be.

•

What superpowers equip you to pursue your passions?

> **Focus on what lights a fire inside you and use that passion to fill a white space.**

KENDRA SCOTT

JEWELRY DESIGNER • CEO

Her story. Your story.

•

Kendra Scott was on forced bed rest during maternity leave when she decided to embark on a venture that would bring together her core passions: family, fashion, and philanthropy. She used the downtime to dream up her first gemstone jewelry collection, rolling $500 of startup capital into a billion-dollar, purpose-filled business that gives back millions each year in funds and volunteer hours to boost wellness, entrepreneurship, and education in each store's local community.

•

Describe a project or experience that lit a fire inside you.
What about it ignited your excitement to learn, see, and do more?

Kendra found her niche by turning the gemstones she adored into dazzling products for good.

•

Have you thought about how you might you use one or more of your passions to fill the "white space" of a gap in the market? Jot your ideas here.

"Try to find the thing you find coolest
even if it seems impossible."

KATIE BOUMAN
COMPUTER SCIENTIST WHO HELPED CREATE THE
FIRST IMAGE OF A BLACK HOLE IN OUTER SPACE

"As you work to find your passion, beware . . .
It might just find you."

CONDOLEEZZA RICE
CONCERT PIANIST TURNED SOVIET EXPERT
TURNED TRAILBLAZING SECRETARY OF STATE

Timeline

Track those moments when you took the plunge and offered up a passionate "yes" to life when it would've been easier to say "no."

I said "yes" to:

_____

_____

_____

_____

_____

Date: ....

I said "yes" to:

_____

_____

_____

_____

_____

Date: ....

I said "yes" to:

_____

_____

_____

_____

_____

Date: ....

I said "yes" to:

_____

_____

_____

_____

_____

Date: ....

I said "yes" to:

_____

_____

_____

_____

_____

Date: ....

I said "yes" to:

_____

_____

_____

_____

_____

Date: ....

"So how can I stay passionate?
I train by saying yes to whatever comes my way: drama, comedy,
tragedy, love, death, losses. Yes to life. And I train by staying in love."

ISABEL ALLENDE
JOURNALIST • BEST-SELLING NOVELIST •
WOMEN'S EMPOWERMENT FOUNDATION FOUNDER

"

Go find your joy. It's what you're going to remember in the end. It's not the worry, it's not the what-ifs. It's the joy that stays with you.

"

SANDRA BULLOCK
ACTOR

Words to live by.

Write down a quote or message (from yourself or someone else) that encourages you to live out your passions.

"I long to accomplish a great and noble task, but it is my chief duty to accomplish small tasks as if they were great and noble."

HELEN KELLER
HUMANITARIAN

•

"Every single one of us makes an impact on the planet every single day, and we get to choose what sort of impact that is."

JANE GOODALL
PRIMATOLOGIST

•

"A dream is a portal to your purpose."

LUPITA NYONG'O
ACTOR

"

For anyone trying to discern
what to do with their life:
PAY ATTENTION TO WHAT
YOU PAY ATTENTION TO.
That's pretty much all the
info you need.

"

AMY KROUSE ROSENTHAL

CHILDREN'S BOOK AUTHOR

Take note.

What do you pay attention to?

Have any unexpected items or patterns emerged from your list?
Run with them.

"

I've never scored a goal in my
life without getting a pass
from someone else.

"

ABBY WAMBACH
PRO SOCCER PLAYER

Your team.

•

To live the life you imagine, you can't go it alone.

•

Who's given you the essential assists for netting your goals?
Who could you draft in for realizing your current dreams?

PARTNERS & COLLABORATORS • FAMILY & FRIENDS • COACHES &
TEAM MEMBERS • SUPPORTERS & FANS • MENTORS & SPONSORS

"

Sow an act and you reap a habit;
sow a habit and you reap
a character; sow a character
and you reap a destiny.

"

FRANCES WILLARD
SOCIAL REFORMER

Seeds of success.

·

Frances Willard was such an effective campaigner, she helped get two amendments added to the US Constitution. As a founder of the temperance movement, she famously pushed for teetotaling, but she was a big believer in the "law of habits" in general, even writing a how-to book for girls with recs such as creating a personal regimen, consciously cultivating positive thinking, and piping up at church meetings to get comfortable with public speaking. We might not all have Frances's level of self-discipline, but we *can* all benefit from rituals, routines, and practices intentionally designed to aid our aims.

·

Do you have any habits or practices that help keep you on track?

"

Declare yourself for a cause.
Because once you declare yourself
for something, it's like you get
your true north, your compass,
your guiding light.

"

CRISTINA MITTERMEIER
CONSERVATION PHOTOGRAPHER

Her story. Your story.

•

Mexico-born marine biologist Cristina Mittermeier let her quest to preserve the world's oceans guide her into pioneering a new field—conservation photography. Even with a set direction, it took years of hard work to navigate to the sweet spot of purpose where she could put a passion of hers in service of the needs of her community and our world.

Cristina had suddenly discovered her talent for taking pictures on a trip to the Amazon rain forest. It also seemed like the perfect tool for sharing her love of nature with the world. The aftermath of her aha moment meant putting in time to get formal training and professional experience before she had the skills and resources to set her own assignments. Today, the bona fide National Geographic explorer uses her wonder-inspiring wildlife photos—snapped while deep-diving underwater or trekking to the world's rarest ecosystems— to invite us to join in her planet-saving adventures.

•

Do you have a "true north"?
Is there a time when you've let a cause steer your course?

Cristina's journey to realize her purpose was in many ways about finding her people. After observing that the scientific papers she wrote as a marine biologist didn't reach the wide audience she needed to spark a movement, she turned to photography as a powerful way to tell the story of our seas and the threats they face. She founded an organization—the International League of Conservation Photographers—to build a supportive network for their mission-driven art. Shooting for National Geographic brought her work to a community aligned with her interests, so that when she was able to cofound the nonprofit she'd long been envisioning, SeaLegacy already had millions of followers ready to hop on board.

·

How might you invite people to join in a mission of yours? Who are they? Where are they?

"Ask for what you want. Define what you want.
If you don't get it where you are, create it."

ROSE MARCARIO

MINDFUL CEO LEADING THE WAY ON SUSTAINABILITY

"Be steady. Stay focused. Remember your purpose.
And, always press forward."

YAMICHE ALCINDOR
LONGTIME REPORTER ON THE POLITICS BEAT TURNED
AWARD-WINNING WHITE HOUSE CORRESPONDENT

Timeline

Purpose is also about planning, about mapping how you get from here to there and parsing out the small, intentional steps that'll help along the way. Use this timeline as a starting point. Name the puzzle pieces you'll need to work on to assemble the big picture.

My goal _____

Knowledge required:	Skills called for:
_____	_____
_____	_____
How I'll attain it:	**How I'll develop them:**
_____	_____
_____	_____
_____	_____
When:	When: ....

Experience demanded:

_____

_____

How I'll get it:

_____

_____

_____

When: ....

Connections to make:

_____

_____

How I'll find them:

_____

_____

_____

When: ....

Resources needed:

_____

_____

Where I'll get them:

_____

_____

_____

When: ....

Collaborators to look for:

_____

_____

Where I'll seek them:

_____

_____

_____

When: ....

"Think big, work small."

PAT SUMMITT

BASKETBALL COACH • 8-TIME NCAA CHAMPION • FOUNDATION FOUNDER

"

Experience has taught me that you cannot value dreams according to the odds of their coming true. Their real value is in stirring within us the will to aspire. That will, wherever it finally leads, does at least move you forward. And after a time you may recognize that the proper measure of success is not how much you've closed the distance to some far-off goal but the quality of what you've done today.

"

SONIA SOTOMAYOR
US SUPREME COURT JUSTICE

Words to live by.

Here's space to write down words (by you or someone else) that reaffirm your sense of purpose or give you a sense of direction.

"The way of progress is neither swift nor easy."

MARIE CURIE
SCIENTIST

•

"It's the rough side of the mountain that's easiest to climb;
the smooth side doesn't have anything for you to hang on to."

ARETHA FRANKLIN
SOUL SINGER

•

"I hate to lose, but losing has brought me here today.
The only reason I am who I am is because of my losses."

SERENA WILLIAMS
PRO TENNIS PLAYER

TENACIOUSLY

endeavor VERVE intention

mettle HARD WORK

MOXIE WILLPOWER

ENDURANCE commitment

tenacity pluck

nerve DEDICATION

PRACTICE a moment of success,
a lifetime of effort

DETERMINATION

stick-with-it-ness

perseverance

resolve

persistence

DRIVE

fortitude RESILIENCE

COMEBACKS GRIT

stamina discipline

Your take.

Think about your tough times and long hauls.
What has tenacity come to mean to you? When do you need it?
Who embodies it? Pen your personal definition or just freely list the
words, people, and things you associate with it.

"

Next time you fail at something or someone leaves you heartbroken . . . let yourself be sad, grieve what didn't happen for a minute, but move ON. Better things are waiting for you.

"

REESE WITHERSPOON
ACTOR-PRODUCER • ENTREPRENEUR

Spill it.

Take a minute to acknowledge those people and things that feel like they're holding you back. Write down anything that comes to mind—

LETDOWNS & SETBACKS • WHAT YOU DON'T KNOW & WHAT YOU DON'T HAVE • HATERS & NAYSAYERS • RULES & REGS • HOLDING PATTERNS & ROADBLOCKS • NAGGING WORRIES & BIG FEARS

Being tenacious means getting past hurdles and moving on.

So now, turn the page.

"

Turn your 'nos' into 'yesses.'

"

DYLLAN MCGEE
DOCUMENTARY MAKER

Her story. Your story.

Some of the worthiest causes and best ideas have faced major resistance and countless rejections along the way. Yet sometimes a "no" can be a gift.

•

When producer Dyllan McGee asked Gloria Steinem to be the subject of a film on feminism, the iconic activist took a pass. Gloria strongly believed you can't even begin to tell the story of a movement through the life of one person. Instead of retreating or stubbornly staying the course, Dyllan let that feedback reshape her vision. In the end, Gloria's refusal led to a much grander idea. It prompted Dyllan to found MAKERS with the aim of creating the world's largest and most diverse video archive of women's stories, told in their own voices. Today it's an established media brand built on empowering historymakers.

•

Describe one moment (or more) when you were able to turn a rejection, refusal, or setback into a positive opportunity.

You've done it before . . .

So how could you turn the nos you're currently facing into yesses?

"Don't let fear get in the way and don't be afraid to say 'I don't know' or 'I don't understand.' . . . And don't always listen to the so-called experts!"

MARGARET HAMILTON

LEAD NASA SOFTWARE ENGINEER ON THE APOLLO MISSIONS TO THE MOON

"Doing work eliminates the need for luck.
I'm not lucky, I just took the stairs. And you should, too."

LILLY SINGH

YOUTUBER TURNED LATE-NIGHT HOST

Timeline

Fill this in for past trip-ups or record them in real time.
Include any that come to mind or use this timeline to track a
specific project.

Trip-up:
_____

I got back up because:
_____
_____
_____
_____

Date: ....

Trip-up:
_____

Here's who helped me through:
_____
_____
_____
_____

Date: ....

Trip-up:
_____

I learned this about myself:
_____
_____
_____
_____

Date: ....

Trip-up:

_____

I found a better way:

_____

_____

_____

_____

Date: ....

Trip-up:

_____

My source of energy has become:

_____

_____

_____

_____

Date: ....

Trip-up:

_____

I'm braver because:

_____

_____

_____

_____

Date: ....

"To be gritty is to keep putting one foot in front of the other. To be gritty is to hold fast to an interesting and purposeful goal. To be gritty is to invest, day after week after year, in challenging practice. To be gritty is to fall down seven times, and rise eight."

ANGELA DUCKWORTH
PSYCHOLOGIST • GRIT RESEARCHER •
CHARACTER LAB FOUNDER

"

I don't need easy,
I just need possible.

"

BETHANY HAMILTON
PRO SURFER

Words to live by.

Here's space to record a quote that keeps you going time and again—
could be your words, could be someone else's . . .
While you're at it, why not save it to your phone, post it at your desk,
hang it on your wall, or share it with a friend?

"

Being perfect is replaceable.
Being unique and individual
is irreplaceable.

"

MERRITT MOORE
QUANTUM PHYSICIST • PRO BALLERINA

SIGNATURE
THINKING

Your ideas.

•

Your story.

•

Your future in the making.

•

It's time to reflect.

•

And share.

Throughout this journal, you've recorded your story and your takes on important themes for anyone's journey, from authenticity to tenacity. Now, it's time to sift out the passages you find most meaningful and craft them into your own shareworthy quotes to carry you forward. This is also a golden opportunity to identify some "signature thinking"—ideas that you'd like to share or words to inspire others while speaking to who you are as a person.

You'll also have the chance to look back on the big idea you revealed in the opening of this journal to see how it may have evolved, been fine-tuned, or taken a radical turn into something new.

Tips for scouting your quotes.

As you look back through what you've written for your best nuggets of wisdom, here are a few things to look for:

Has a personal mantra emerged?

A FRAMEWORTHY EXAMPLE:

When UN diplomat Christiana Figueres was heading up the years-long negotiations to broker the first major global deal to curb climate change, she ended up hanging the motto "Impossible is not a fact; it's an attitude." on her office wall.

·

Is there a moment from your story that resonates beyond its context?

AN AVIATION ILLUSTRATION:

When pilot turned astronaut Susan Helms asked herself, "How can I fly higher and faster than I am doing now?" it was a literal question—she wanted to trade her plane for a rocket. But it's also a question that we can all ask ourselves in a symbolic sort of way—how can we push ourselves to get to the next level?

·

Did your response to a personal question prompt wisdom that echoes more widely?

AN UNREHEARSED ANSWER:

American Ballet Theatre principal dancer Misty Copeland was asked how she stays humble in spite of her celebrity status. She cited the relentless hard work she has to put in at the studio to stay on "pointe." Her grounding statement, "We are only as good as our last performance," could apply equally to any profession.

Does one of your takeaways capture your unique voice or perspective?

A SALTY SAMPLE:

Poet Mary Karr told college grads, "Being smart and rich are lucky, but being curious and compassionate will save your ass," putting her funny, frank, no-nonsense demeanor on display.

·

Could you communicate an idea in a way that helps tell your story?

A SWEET SAMPLE:

When entrepreneur Martha Stewart wrote, "So, the pie isn't perfect? Cut it in wedges," she offered life advice that speaks to her status as star baker and lifestyle guru who's deftly handled many a pie-cutting crisis.

PLUS, THIS HOME RUN:

Barrier-breaker Linda Alvarado, the construction firm founder who's co-owner of the Colorado Rockies pro baseball team, pitched her counsel on risk-taking in a memorable way by using the language of her "field": "You are never going to get to second base if you keep your foot safely on first."

66

It's about letting your true self speak.
It's about seeing your voice as an
instrument and learning to play it right.

99

SUSAN CAIN
LAWYER TURNED ADVOCATE FOR INTROVERTS

Making your quotes sing.

"Exactly!"
That's the response you'll hear when you've clarified an idea with your words and the story behind them.

Quotable quotes come in many forms: uncommon insights, plainspoken thinking, in-the-moment responses, or deep-rooted wisdom packed with layers of meaning. But there are things that make some resonate more than others.

Here are a few questions—based on our years of research on which words hit home—you might consider as you draft your own quotations:

• Is it short?

• Is it pithy?

• Are the words or how you combine them unique enough to grab attention?

• Does it stand-alone? That is, can it be understood without knowing the context?

• Does it express your voice and personality?

• Is it written how you'd speak it?

• Is it spoken how you'd actually say it?

• Does it connect back to your story?

Don't be hard on yourself. Some of the most eloquent leaders had speechwriters to weave magic from words. Some of our most prolific writers have spent their entire lives honing the art of spinning language into a rich host of meanings and emotions. Your ideas are your ideas. And you'll draft them, live with them, finesse them—so they mean something to you. With your story behind the words, they might just resonate with one other person, a community, or beyond. But for that to happen, you have to put yourself out there. So start somewhere.

Here's space to noodle with your signature ideas.

Now, fill the designed pages that follow with your very own words,
and, when you're ready, share them with the world.
(P.S. Don't forget to take credit by adding your name and
a title or two that gives a sense of who you are.
That way your idea will be properly cited.)

"

"

Big idea.
REVISITED

Date

_____

My thinking + doing has evolved my "someday" dream into this . . .

"No fairy tales. Be your own narrator.
And go for a happy ending."

SHONDA RHIMES
SHOWRUNNER

Quoteur list & bio bits

quoteur / KWÖ TəR / noun
A person who originates a collection of words worth sharing.

We believe the stories behind the quotations make the ideas more powerful. What follows is a glimpse at the lives behind the lines featured in this journal—the people whose words, titles, or deeds stoked your imagination, challenged your intellect, or echoed your heart. You'll also be surprised how many women are behind historic and modern-day inventions, products, brands, and bold ventures. Our hope is that you find a new muse ... plus a few movies, books, podcasts, sites, and places to add to your list.

In a sea of misattributions, we're committed to ensuring quotes come from legit sources and to giving credit where credit is due. You can find the citation for each *Bravely* quotation at our digital inspiration gallery, quotabelle.com.

SYLVIA ACEVEDO • born 1957 • the leading scout turned Girl Scouts leader
This onetime rocket scientist credits her Brownie troop leader with introducing her to the wonders of the night sky. She also credits Girl Scouts with empowering her—a Latina with humble roots—to shoot for the stars as an engineer, software entrepreneur, Silicon Valley tech exec, and award-winning education campaigner. She helped other kids follow her stellar lead as CEO of Girl Scouts USA. In her own words: *Path to the Stars.*

HALIMA ADEN • born 1997 • the first hijab-wearing top model
The arc of this Somali American model's story has taken her from a Kenyan refugee camp to the covers of elite fashion magazines. Halima's bold decision to own her identity as a Muslim woman who prefers modest dress has landed her a high-flying career on her own terms. It has also made the industry more inclusive while giving her a platform for philanthropy as a UNICEF ambassador. In her own words: her *Glamour* editorial for the 2019 World Refugee Day.

YAMICHE ALCINDOR • born 1986 • the journalist standing up for freedom of the press

A Florida native with Haitian-born parents, Yamiche reaffirmed her interest in journalism following an internship with the *Miami Herald* at age 16. She's earned her chops handling tense assignments for prestigious media outlets, calling upon her ability to speak Haitian Creole and French to unearth stories of humanity during the 2010 earthquake in Haiti and bolstering her belief in the Fourth Estate while covering a contentious White House during the coronavirus pandemic. See her on: *PBS NewsHour.*

ISABEL ALLENDE • born 1942 • the writer of "tales of passion"

Isabel was a journalist in political exile from her native Chile when news that her 100-year-old grandfather was on his deathbed prompted her to pen her first best-selling novel, *The House of Spirits*. Now with a National Book Award and more than 20 titles to her name, she's one of the world's most widely read Spanish-language authors. Look up her TED Talks for tips on staying passionate or read her heartbreaking ode to her late daughter, *Paula*, for wisdom about coping with loss.

LINDA ALVARADO • born 1951 • the high-rise builder

Credited with helping to break the "concrete ceiling," this trailblazing construction exec founded her own commercial and general contracting firm in 1976. Linda built her business from the ground floor by winning bids for sidewalks and bus shelters. Today, her portfolio includes schools, stadiums, convention centers, and high-rises. The Denver resident's investment in the Colorado Rockies also made her the first Hispanic owner in Major League Baseball. To watch: Linda on the first season of PBS's *Makers*.

MAYA ANGELOU • 1928–2014 • the "phenomenal woman"

A precocious child rendered mute by abuse, Maya rose up when she dared to share her story. The sometimes waitress, dancer, streetcar conductor, and paint remover became an internationally renowned author and humanitarian. Besides publishing 30+ best sellers, including everything from poetry to cookbooks, she wrote herself into the history books as a beloved beacon of wit and wisdom. Her masterpiece: *I Know Why the Caged Bird Sings*. Also: *Letters to My Daughter*.

IRIS APFEL • born 1921 • the self-styled "geriatric starlet"

Long a successful interior designer with a textile firm she ran with her husband, Iris was launched into the limelight after an exhibit at the Met showcased her fabulously loud and unique wardrobe and the subsequent documentary *Iris* captured her matching outsize personality. "My overnight took seven decades," she jokes—proof it's never too late to be a style icon . . . or get a modeling contract! In her own words: *Iris Apfel, Accidental Icon.*

JACINDA ARDERN • born 1980 • the empathetic head of state

In the first few years of her tenure as New Zealand's prime minister, Jacinda has dealt with a deadly terrorist attack, volcanic eruption, and global pandemic (all while caring for a newborn baby). Her unstinting compassion, strength, and competence in the face of crisis have garnered her international attention as a fresh face of true leadership. To watch: her speech at the Christchurch Memorial.

CLAIRE BABINEAUX-FONTENOT • born 1964 • the compassionate CEO

This onetime tax attorney and Walmart EVP is now the head of the second-largest charity in the US. Growing up with more than 100 adopted and fostered siblings, Claire often saw the effects of malnutrition firsthand when new brothers and sisters arrived at their home. Today, she's bringing her business savvy to the front lines of hunger relief as CEO of Feeding America, overseeing programs that serve 47 million people a year while ensuring healthful fresh foods end up in kitchens instead of landfills. To visit: Feeding America's website.

GERTRUDE BELL • 1868–1926 • the "Queen of the Desert"

An English explorer ahead of her time, Gertrude trekked through the Middle East to pursue her penchant for ancient archaeology. Besides writing travel books, learning to speak six languages, making maps, and helping to found a museum in Baghdad, Gertrude aided British intelligence during WWI and afterward served as the only influential female policy adviser and official in the region. In her own words: *A Woman in Arabia.*

KATIE BOUMAN • born 1989 • the imager of the impossible-to-see

As a grad student, this computational imaging whiz (with no background in astronomy) was brought on to the Event Horizon Telescope team to help perform a task that had long been thought impossible—getting a picture of one of the universe's most mysterious phenomena: a black hole. With the aid of her coding, they did. Today, the Caltech prof is rejoining the team to produce an image of the black hole at the heart of our own Milky Way. See her on: TED or Caltech on YouTube.

BRENÉ BROWN • born 1965 • the prof spreading bravery with data & stories

A social work researcher and "recovering perfectionist," Brené has become a modern prophet for courageous, wholehearted living based on embracing our authentic, vulnerable selves. Since delivering one of TED's most popular talks, she's put out a series of best-selling books and even her own Netflix special, *The Call to Courage.* Some of her most popular work (along with her own personal philosophy) is inspired by a Theodore Roosevelt quote—a challenge to *Dare Greatly.*

SANDRA BULLOCK • born 1964 • the actor dubbed "America's Sweetheart"
This Oscar-winning superstar got her start in showbiz by lending her voice to the children's choruses of operas her singer mother had roles in. Her winning top-billed performances in action flicks like *Speed* and rom-coms like *Miss Congeniality* made her box-office gold and among the world's highest-paid actresses. A heartwarming watch: her surprise 2014 graduation speech at Warren Easton Charter High School in her adopted home of New Orleans, Louisiana.

SUSAN CAIN • born 1968 • the quiet revolutionary
Once a successful corporate lawyer, this advocate for introverts left her legal career to give a voice to her community. Her best-selling book—seven years in the making—*Quiet* made waves by arguing for the value of soft-and-silent leadership in a culture that tends to lionize extroverts. It also catalyzed a movement to help other introverts realize their potential by putting her insights into practice in homes, schools, and workplaces. To visit: quietrev.com.

JULIA CAMERON • born 1948 • the all-around artist
She has written plays and screenplays, penned poems and novels, composed music and lyrics, made and directed films, but this prolific creative is probably best known for helping unblock others' creativity. Julia's magnum opus, *The Artist's Way*, offers a spiritually driven inventory of tools for imagining, experimenting, and creating. *Walking in This World* and *Finding Water* are among her motivating follow-ups.

JULIA CHILD • 1912–2004 • the "French Chef" & cooking show pioneer
When Julia's husband (a fellow US WWII intelligence officer) was posted to France, the move opened her eyes to the wonders of continental cuisine. Her dauntless attitude and infectiously fun personality helped her become its chief proponent in the US with wildly popular TV programs and cookbooks that earned her three Emmys plus a National Book Award and countless foodie fans. Today, a replica of Julia's famous kitchen is enshrined as an exhibit at the Smithsonian Institution's National Museum of American History in Washington DC. In her own words: *Julia's Kitchen Wisdom*.

PEMA CHÖDRÖN • born 1936 • the guiding light of contemporary spirituality
This onetime English teacher turned to Buddhism to seek spiritual answers after a series of personal heartbreaks. Eventually ordained as a nun in the Vajrayana tradition, Pema also became the inaugural director of Gampo Abbey, North America's first Tibetan monastery for Westerners. People of all beliefs turn to her writings for guidance on coping with loss and uncertainty. Classics include *When Things Fall Apart* and the handbook *Start Where You Are*.

BARBE-NICOLE PONSARDIN CLICQUOT • 1777–1866 • the grande dame of champagne

Widow Clicquot transformed a failing family-owned French vineyard into an innovative champagne house celebrated for spurring worldwide demand for bottles of bubbly. Her invention of "riddling" in the early 1800s (still in use today), shook the waste out of costly production processes, while her keen business mind helped her become one of the earliest-known global businesswomen. Barbe-Nicole's namesake brand remains among champagne's best sellers. To enjoy: Veuve Clicquot.

MISTY COPELAND • born 1982 • the "unlikely ballerina"

Misty discovered her hidden passion and talent for ballet at her local Boys & Girls Club. At 13, she was a late bloomer in the dance world who never fit its traditional pale and waiflike ideal. The driven prodigy put in two difficult decades at the barre to become American Ballet Theatre's first African American principal dancer. Her unique brand of graceful strength has seen her make the leap to pop culture sensation. In her own words: *Life in Motion*. To help children forge their own "unlikely" paths: *Firebird*.

DOMINIQUE CRENN • born 1965 • the culinary poet

This aspiring chef left her native France for San Francisco to enter the male-dominated domain of fine dining. Without any formal training, she went on to become the US's first woman to earn three Michelin stars for Atelier Crenn, where daily menus take the form of poetry and the dishes are just as artful. Her recent memoir *Rebel Chef* is a tantalizing taste of her search for what matters through food and activism.

MARIE CURIE • 1867–1934 • the "First Lady of Science"

An indefatigable researcher, Marie added two elements to the periodic table while helping to write the book on radioactivity, the phenomenon underlying technologies from x-rays to carbon dating. Leaving occupied Poland to study in Paris, Marie became the Sorbonne's first female professor and lab head . . . not to mention, the first person to win two Nobel Prizes—one for physics, one for chemistry. Marie's personal papers will be radioactive for another 1,500 years, but you can access her intimate insights in the biography she wrote of her husband and collaborator, *Pierre Curie*.

MARY DALY • 1928–2010 • the philosopher of courageous conviction

Born into a Roman Catholic family, this prominent theologian spent her academic career critiquing traditional religion. Her controversial, no-holds-barred ideas kindled important debates and won many accolades. An animal rights activist and feminist, she spent 33 years as a college professor, famously excluding men from her courses to create a safe space for female students to think and grow. To ponder, her proclamation: "God is a Verb."

VIOLA DAVIS • born 1965 • the Oscar, Emmy, two-time Tony winning actor
Viola has earned the entertainment industry's highest honors, a testament to a career where she hasn't shied away from soul-bearing, complex characters. But it's not awards she's in search of; it's significance. Shaping a legacy that leaves her feeling she's been leading with intention and meaning in her life's work is the essence of her focus these days. To watch: Viola's 2017 Oscar acceptance speech (and the film *Fences*).

ANGELA DUCKWORTH • born 1970 • the psychologist of success
Angela was teaching seventh-grade math when she wondered why the students she considered to be the most gifted were rarely the highest achievers. Now a psychology prof whose research is backed by the MacArthur and Gates Foundations, she's got the data-backed answer—hard work and self-discipline trump IQ and talent as predictors of success. Read about her findings in the book *Grit* or look up the site of her nonprofit Character Lab for playbooks to encourage a growth mindset.

REGINA DUGAN • born 1963 • the unfettered inventor
As the first female head of the US Pentagon's innovation engine, DARPA, this business exec and tech developer won props for motivating her team to go for long-shot projects. Their fearless experimentation led to everything from portable land mine detection devices to hummingbird drones to thought-powered prosthetic arms. Since leaving government, Regina's brought her blue-sky leadership to heavy hitters like Google and Facebook. See her on: TED.

SYLVIA EARLE • born 1935 • the adventurous oceanographer dubbed "Her Deepness"
This groundbreaking marine biologist has logged more than 7,000 hours underwater exploring largely uncharted reaches of our oceans. Today, the first female head of the US National Oceanic and Atmospheric Association is a full-time environmentalist whose nonprofit Mission Blue is seeking to create protected marine zones. Dip into books *Blue Hope* and *The World Is Blue* for a peek at the wonders Sylvia's trying to conserve.

TINA ROTH EISENBERG • born 1974 • the avid serial entrepreneur
This Swiss-born designer arrived in New York City with a modern design sensibility and heaps of enthusiasm, launching a blog that she called her personal visual archive and a memorable handle: swissmiss. Her infectious spirit parlayed her work into a Brooklyn-based design studio turned coworking space plus a host of other ventures. To follow: @swissmiss. To attend: CreativeMornings.

LOUISE ERDRICH • born 1954 • the multidimensional storyteller

An enrolled member of the Turtle Mountain Band of Chippewa, Louise is known for her lyrical literary explorations of her Native American and German American roots told from multiple viewpoints. Her 28 titles feature memoirs, poetry, and children's literature, but she's most famous for novels, like her National Book Award winner *The Round House*. Her indie bookstore in Minneapolis, Minnesota, doubles as a hub for fellow Native American authors. A favorite: her poem "Advice to Myself."

CHRISTIANA FIGUERES • born 1956 • the planet-saving optimist

This Costa Rican and United Nations diplomat was the "force of nature" behind the world's first-ever comprehensive agreement on addressing climate change. The deal took six years to negotiate, but it's the only time 195 countries have jointly signed on to anything. Christiana trained as an anthropologist but became interested in environmental issues when she learned a species she loved as kid—the golden toad—had gone extinct by the time her daughters were born. See her on: TED. Hear her on: the podcast she cohosts, *Outrage + Optimism*.

LOUISE FILI • born 1951 • the retro-modern graphic design studio founder

Louise is among the most esteemed modern-day experts in the art of typography. At 16, she sent away for her first calligraphy pen, and then practiced and practiced, igniting a lifelong passion for lettering and design. Vintage signs from her family's native Italy influenced her elegant aesthetic. Her work can be seen in books and on postal stamps, food labels, restaurant signage, and more. For eye candy & inspiration, read: *Elegantissima*.

ARETHA FRANKLIN • 1942–2018 • the "Queen of Soul"

A preacher's kid who grew up singing gospel in church, Aretha belted her way through a rocky adolescence on the road to become a blues and soul legend. With anthems like "Think" and "Respect," she won 18 Grammys, performed at two US presidential inaugurations, and was the Rock & Roll Hall of Fame's first female inductee. Topping the charts throughout the civil rights era, she was still trending into her 70s. To watch: National Geographic's *Genius: Aretha*.

MELINDA GATES • born 1964 • the data-driven philanthropist

Once a young techie marketing manager who helped develop Microsoft's multimedia offerings, Melinda has brought that spirit of disruptive innovation to philanthropy as the head of the world's largest private charitable organization. The Bill & Melinda Gates Foundation has made serious dents in health care, education, social policy, and global development while backing projects with big impacts, like finding a coronavirus vaccine. To read: her manifesto for global gender equality, *The Moment of Lift*.

SIMONE GIERTZ • born 1990 • the self-taught tech maker

An engineering school dropout, Simone earned a fan following with a series of videos showcasing useless inventions that hilariously misfire in their everyday applications (think: mechanical arm smearing lipstick all over her face). Since being confronted with an unwanted "plot twist"—a brain tumor that required surgery and radiation—the "Queen of Shitty Robots" has decided to renounce her crown to claim the title: serious innovator. Her first big project? Creating the electric pickup truck not yet available on the market. To watch: Simone Giertz's channel on YouTube.

GABBY GIFFORDS • born 1970 • the survivor spreading resilience

This former US congressperson became a nationally recognized gun control advocate after surviving a shooting that left six dead in her Arizona constituency. Her courageous recovery from the traumatic brain injury that left her with impaired speech and vision has inspired the nation, as has her continued commitment to public service. In her own words: *Gabby*.

ELIZABETH GILBERT • born 1969 • the journey-inspiring memoirist

This adventurous author had a literary breakthrough with her best-selling book turned cultural touchstone, a travel memoir about coming back from a divorce-incited spiritual crisis. The two-time movie muse (*Eat, Pray, Love* and *Coyote Ugly*) has helped countless others dare to unlock their full creative potential with works of nonfiction like *Big Magic* and her podcast *Magic Lessons*.

JANE GOODALL • born 1934 • the primatologist and beloved eco-warrior

At age 26 with no formal training, Jane scored her dream job observing chimpanzees in Africa's Gombe Reserve. Her decades of fascinating fieldwork have made her the foremost expert on and advocate for chimpanzees . . . not to mention a dame, UN messenger of peace, and one of the world's best-known scientists. Her nonprofit Jane Goodall Institute has offices in 25 countries while her Roots & Shoots youth program has 8,000 chapters. To watch: *Jane Goodall: The Hope*. To watch for: the unrelenting optimist's latest—*The Book of Hope*.

AMANDA GORMAN • born 1998 • the US's inaugural youth poet laureate

In spite of having a speech impediment, this LA spoken-word poet has become a voice of her generation, performing everywhere from the UN to the White House. She won hearts with a riveting, hope-raising televised rendition of her poem "The Miracle of Morning," written in response to the coronavirus pandemic. Already a published author and literacy nonprofit founder, she's committed to a presidential run in 2036.

MARTHA GRAHAM • 1894–1991 • "Mother of Modern Dance"

The most influential dancer of the 20th century, Martha introduced a stark new style of movement designed to express the raw core of human experience. She founded her own company and school, choreographed 181 avant-garde ballets, and graced the stage well into her 70s. Look up Agnes De Mille's *Martha* for interviews that showcase the artist's provocative philosophies about creativity and life.

TIFFANY HADDISH • born 1979 • the breakout comedy star

This onetime foster kid found her calling to be a comedian when a social worker sent her to a Laugh Factory summer camp for underprivileged youth. Still, Tiffany had to grind for two decades to hit the big time with her scene-stealing debut in the movie *Girls Trip*. Soon after she made history (and earned an Emmy) as the first black woman stand-up to host *SNL*. In her own words: *The Last Black Unicorn*.

ZAHA HADID • 1950–2016 • the "Queen of the Curve"

This Iraqi-born starchitect wowed the world with her ultramodern yet organic designs, from curvy asymmetrical skyscrapers to fluid "fields" of buildings that defy distinctions between inside and out. After founding her own London studio, the trailblazer became the first woman to win the highest honor in her profession: the Pritzker Architecture Prize. To visit: Google Arts & Culture's virtual tours of Zaha's most iconic buildings, from Beijing's Galaxy Soho complex to London's Olympic Aquatics Centre.

BETHANY HAMILTON • born 1990 • the never-give-up athlete

At age 13, this aspiring pro surfer lost her left arm after being attacked by a 14-foot tiger shark. Within a month, Bethany was back on her board, more determined than ever to pursue her dream. She won her first national competition two years later, and she's still carving waves at the top of her sport today, even when that's meant nursing her two young sons between heats. Her epic comeback and abiding faith have left a wake of inspiration. To watch: the documentary *Unstoppable*.

MARGARET HAMILTON • born 1936 • the original software engineer

If this young mathematician turned computer scientist would have listened to the so-called experts, Neil Armstrong might never have landed on the moon. Always attracted to things that have never been done before, Margaret signed on to lead the NASA team of 100 tasked with creating the flight guidance software for the Apollo missions. Her trailblazing work came off with zero bugs. In the process, she coined a job title that's only too familiar today: software engineer. In her own words: her 2016 interview with *Futurism*.

SIMONE HANNAH-CLARK • born 1980 • the steadfast "builder"

This New Zealand-born intensive care nurse was working in a Brooklyn hospital when it was suddenly overwhelmed with COVID-19 patients. Her firsthand accounts of the "battle" against the pandemic provided heart-wrenching insights into the experiences of those on the front lines of the crisis. Simone's heartening words also showed how nurses are not "handmaidens or angels" but tough, skilled professionals ready to meet unprecedented calamity with unstinting care. In her own words: "An ICU Nurse's Coronavirus Diary" in the *New York Times*.

SUSAN HELMS • born 1958 • the ultimate high-flyer

When Susan enlisted in the US Air Force straight out of high school, she had no idea she'd someday fly as high as the International Space Station. During the pilot and engineer's 12-year career at NASA, she clocked 211 days in space on five missions. Susan eventually retired from the military as a three-star general and still holds the record for the longest space walk (eight hours and 56 minutes). To visit: Susan's display in the US Astronaut Hall of Fame at the Kennedy Space Center in Florida.

MELLODY HOBSON • born 1969 • the "color brave" champion

From humble roots in Chicago, Mellody started as an intern at Ariel Investments and worked her way up to become president of the largest minority-owned firm. Besides shattering stereotypes as one of the few women on many a high-powered board, like Starbucks and DreamWorks Animation, she's emerged as a leader on the difficult-to-discuss issue of race relations, urging us to find the courage to "go there" together. See her on: TED.

MAE JEMISON • born 1956 • the first African American woman in space

This young Trekkie grew up with cosmic ambitions to board her own rocket ship. After a stint as a Peace Corps medical officer in Africa, the physician's dream came true when NASA selected her to be a mission specialist on the *Endeavor* shuttle. Today, the prominent STEM advocate has an even more sci-fi goal: building a "starship" to travel beyond our solar system. On a side note: it was one of Mae's quotes and her story that inspired our own mission at Quotabelle. To listen: A Conversation with Dr. Mae Jemison on *StarTalk*.

KATHERINE JOHNSON • 1918–2020 • the mathematician who shot for the moon

This math prodigy was one of the unsung women from the early days of NASA who helped launch the first astronauts into space. Braving the many hurdles she faced as a black woman, Katherine earned kudos for her critical calculations of shuttle orbits and became the first woman credited as an author on a Flight Research Division report. Her extraordinary story was among those beautifully told in the hit book and film *Hidden Figures*.

FRIDA KAHLO • 1907–1954 • the modern art icon

Frida became one of the world's most widely recognized artists with her vibrant, often shocking self-portraits that boldly represented personal traumas—such as childhood polio, a bone-shattering bus crash, heartbreaks, and miscarriages. The Mexican painter's wholly distinctive styles in both art and fashion made her a groundbreaker in her day and an enduring mainstay of popular culture. In her own words: *The Diary of Frida Kahlo*.

ROSABETH MOSS KANTER • born 1943 • the innovation expert

Rosabeth is a social scientist who has helped leaders across industries take on heady challenges. A longtime prof who became Harvard Business School's first female endowed chair, she encourages students to investigate culture, change, and innovation within organizations. Her astute insights resonate as much with aspiring entrepreneurs as they do with those at the helm of corporate giants. Her latest: *Think Outside the Building*.

MARY KARR • born 1955 • the poet who redefined the art of the memoir

Mary is best known as the memoirist who helped revive the genre with *The Liars' Club*, her best-selling account of her less-than-idyllic childhood in a Texas oil town. Today, the kid whose main ambition was to stay out of jail has become a famous writer, award-winning poet, and literature professor. In her own potent, frank, and funny words: *Lit*. A must-watch: her 2015 commencement address at Syracuse University.

HELEN KELLER • 1880–1968 • the storied champion of the American Foundation for the Blind

After an illness left her deaf and blind, this troubled child went on, with the help of her dedicated teacher Anne Sullivan, to become one of the world's most quotable and best-known humanitarians. The first deaf-blind college grad and a prolific writer and speaker, Helen forever changed attitudes toward people with disabilities at a time when institutionalization was the norm. Her autobiography is a classic, and her essay "Optimism" remains a must-read.

ALICIA KEYS • born 1981 • the platinum R&B artist

The gift of a free piano when she was a kid helped set Alicia's course. Her undeniable talent had record companies waging bidding wars to sign her before she'd even graduated from high school. As a total-package artist who writes, performs, and produces her own songs, she picked the label that gave her most creative freedom. Being free to soulfully express herself has netted her 15 Grammys. In her own words: *More Myself*.

JULIET KINCHIN • born 1956 • the cutting-edge curator

Juliet has been the curator of architecture and design for the Museum of Modern Art in New York City for over a decade. The exhibits she's spearheaded and books she's inked help us resee art and everyday objects we take for granted—from typeforms to sugar cubes to children's toys—as breakthrough moments in modern design. It's a way of telling history she hopes will get people thinking about how designs express our values . . . plus catalyze the creative breakthroughs of tomorrow. To visit: Virtual Views of MoMA.

BARBARA KINGSOLVER • born 1955 • the STEM-inspired author

Aided by a scholarship, Barbara set out from her home in rural Kentucky to study music in college. A wave of pragmatism saw her change course from concert pianist to evolutionary biologist to science communicator until a short story contest launched her career as a celebrated novelist known for characters that find hope in the most challenging circumstances. Her masterpiece: *The Poisonwood Bible*. To watch: her 2008 commencement address at Duke University.

BEYONCÉ KNOWLES • born 1981 • the girl who runs the world

The highest-paid black recording artist of all time, this megastar of the entertainment industry is the only person to have their first six albums debut at #1. From her first talent contest at age seven, this legendary triple threat (singer-songwriter-dancer) kept betting on herself until she had become a bona fide pop icon. Today, Queen Bey has added the titles producer, actor, entrepreneur, CEO, and activist to her repertoire. To watch: *Homecoming*.

ELISABETH KÜBLER-ROSS • 1926–2004 • the "Five Stages of Grief" pioneer

Growing up in Switzerland, Elisabeth's father vehemently opposed her dream of becoming a doctor. She ended up working as a maid. Serving as a frontline helper aiding victims of Nazi Germany paved the way for her history-making role as the renowned psychiatrist that revolutionized how we process grief and support loved ones afflicted with terminal illnesses. Her definitive work: *On Death & Dying*. A wonderful coauthored follow-up on life & living: *Life Lessons*.

SARAH LEWIS • born 1979 • the advocate for artful failure

Sarah's career in art began at 14 when a still life of hers took top honors in an NAACP competition. (Rosa Parks was at the awards ceremony!) Since then, the professor and curator has switched to the history side of the field, studying African American photography and writing the popular book *The Rise* on how innovation and creativity are really about the long-game process of embracing failure and striving for mastery. See her on: TED.

WANGARI MAATHAI • 1940–2011 • the Nobel Peace Prize laureate known as "Africa's Forest Goddess"

Wangari was a Kenyan environmental activist. Originally, her "little" idea to enlist village women as paid tree planters was scoffed at by officials. Today, her heroic efforts are heralded for creating wins on multiple fronts. The Green Belt Movement she founded has resulted in the planting of more than 51 million trees, helping to fight erosion, reverse the devastating impacts of deforestation, reduce Africa's dependency on export crops, and economically empower rural communities. To listen: an inspiring folktale told in her own words "I will be a hummingbird."

ROSE MARCARIO • born 1965 • the activist CEO

A spiritual reckoning led this successful senior exec at a private equity firm to leave her job to seek a role where she could be her "whole self." Rose found exactly that as CEO of Patagonia, where her radical moves to make the gear company even more sustainable have actually boosted its bottom line while inspiring other businesses to follow suit. Now, she's encouraging others to carve out professional lives that combine their passions and values. To listen: "Is Activism Good Business?" from the Aspen Institute's podcast.

BRIDGET "BIDDY" MASON • 1818–1891 • the selfless, self-made philanthropist

Born into slavery, Biddy successfully petitioned for her own freedom in a California court before going on to become one of LA's wealthiest women. Saving her earnings as a mid-wife, she set herself up as a real estate entrepreneur who made sure her investments paid dividends to her community. Her many inspiring deeds included establishing an orphanage, day care center, elementary school, and the First African Methodist Episcopal Church. To see her legacy in action, look up: The Biddy Mason Charitable Foundation.

DYLLAN MCGEE • born 1971 • the documentary innovator

When she was starting out, Dyllan turned down a dream internship at the *Today* show to work at a small production company. Two decades later she'd become an award-winning documentary maker and a partner in the company. Today, the visionary and driven story-teller known as "Relentless McGee" is amplifying women's voices with innovative digital projects and empowerment conferences. To follow: @MAKERSwomen. To attend: The Makers Conference.

MARYAM MIRZAKHANI • 1977–2017 • the geometry genius

Maryam discovered her love of numbers in high school, and by 17 was winning internat-ional math competitions. Her Harvard thesis solved a problem that had stumped pros for years; her breakthrough formulas as a prof made her the first woman to nab math's most prestigious award: the Fields Medal. Not afraid to creatively mix disciplines to pursue big, long-game ideas, her legacy is a reminder: "It's not only the question, but the way you try to solve it."

CRISTINA MITTERMEIER • born 1966 • the conservation photographer

Though an urban girl born in Mexico City, Cristina was always a nature lover. She studied marine biology and got a job cataloguing coastal wildlife before taking up a camera on the hunch that visual communication creates personal connections to science critical to spreading conservation messages. Now a pro photographer and adventurer, she uses her images and nonprofit SeaLegacy to invite people to join the tide of change. To follow on Instagram: @sealegacy, @mitty.

MERRITT MOORE • born 1988 • the "quantum ballerina"

Little girls can now be seen in photos sporting lab coats with toe shoes because they've found a modern-day role model in Merritt. She didn't abandon her dream of dancing ballet with a professional troupe to become a quantum physicist. Instead, she found that spending her days alternating between lab and barre kept both passions fresh. Her next realistic bold dream? Becoming the first person to dance ballet in space. To read: her April 2020 interview with *Vogue UK*.

STEVIE NICKS • born 1948 • the poetic chart-topper

Stevie's original vocals and gift for musical storytelling (not to mention her mythical stage persona and boho style) saw her hit multi-platinum status and has kept her on today's playlists. She's the first woman to be a two-time Rock & Roll Hall of Fame inductee—the first for Fleetwood Mac, a band that epitomized the '70s music scene, and the second for her vast contributions to the music industry as a solo performer. To watch: early videos of Fleetwood Mac performing "Rhiannon" and "Landslide" . . . for Stevie's lyrics and a glimpse at her signature twirl.

FLORENCE NIGHTINGALE • 1820–1910 • the founder of modern nursing

Famous for her compassionate treatment of wounded soldiers during the Crimean War, this British nurse went on to improve the field of medicine as a whole. She wrote a definitive textbook for nurses, founded a school to legitimize the profession, and used her savvy as a statistician to push for widespread hospital reforms to tackle unsanitary conditions. Look up "Florence Nightingale is a Design Hero" on Medium to see how the public health luminary pioneered data visualization with pie charts and infographics that helped curb the spread of deadly diseases.

JACQUELINE NOVOGRATZ • born 1961 • the impact investor

Following her path as a leading social entrepreneur, Jacqueline left Wall Street for Rwanda, helping to set up its first microfinance institution before returning to the US to found a game-changing NGO. Acumen, a "nonprofit venture capital fund for the poor," backs innovation where it's needed most. Its investments in agriculture, education, clean energy, and health care have improved the lives of 200 million people. To watch: two TED Talks. To read: *Manifesto for a Moral Revolution*.

LUPITA NYONG'O • born 1983 • the dreamer who went for it

Watching *The Color Purple* inspired Lupita to chase the improbable dream of being an actor. At 25, the Kenyan student took the risk of auditioning for Yale's legendary drama program. She not only got in; she won an Oscar for her first film role out of the gates as Patsey in *12 Years a Slave*. Since then, Lupita has continued to live her dream, from *Americanah* to *Black Panther*. To look up: her keynote "The Personal Investment in Following a Dream."

ROSA PARKS • 1913–2005 • the movement catalyst

The arrest of this mild-mannered Alabama seamstress famously set off the successful Montgomery bus boycott that was a major boon to the civil rights movement. An NAACP activist trained in nonviolent resistance from the get-go, Rosa continued her advocacy, especially with urban youth, until her death. Today, a statue of her in the US Capitol is a testament to her enduring status as one of the country's most admired historical figures. In her own words: *Rosa Parks, My Story*.

AMY POEHLER • born 1971 • the collaborative comic genius

This onetime improv artist became a household name when she was tapped to join the cast of *SNL*. It didn't take long for her to become a darling of American comedy as she fronted her own fan-favorite sitcom *Parks and Recreation*, starred in many a hit movie, cohosted fabulously funny award shows, and wrote her irreverently wise memoir *Yes Please*. Now she's added producer and nonprofit founder to her repertoire. To follow: @amypoehlersmartgirls.

SHONDA RHIMES • born 1970 • the entertainment industry "badass"

A committed "doer," this powerhouse screenwriter and producer was the first African American woman to have a top-10 network TV show with the addictive medical drama *Grey's Anatomy*. Since then, the hits have kept on coming with series that have brought much-needed diversity to the small screen, not to mention a host of fierce, fascinating, multifaceted female leads. Look up *Year of Yes* for her insights on the life-changing power of one little word.

CONDOLEEZZA RICE • born 1954 • the first African American woman secretary of state

As a kid growing up in a deeply segregated Alabama city, Condoleezza couldn't sip soda at the same counter as a white person, but she'd go on to become a top adviser at the White House. The accomplished Soviet expert discovered her passion for political science in a course taught by Madeleine Albright's father. Now, she's the educator with plenty of hands-on experience who's grooming the next generation of leaders. In her own words: *Extraordinary, Ordinary People*.

ROBIN ROBERTS • born 1960 • the sportscaster & awareness-raising TV anchor

When this breast cancer survivor found out her cancer had come back, it challenged her instinctual optimism. She rallied by leaning on those she loved and living her mother's advice to "make your mess your message." The beloved *Good Morning America* anchor bravely let cameras chronicle her treatment to give others hope and strength. Read about what she learned from the experience in *Everybody's Got Something*.

ANITA RODDICK • 1942–2007 • the "Queen of Green"

As founder of The Body Shop, the British-born Anita was unquestionably a cosmetics giant. She was also a forerunner of ethical consumerism, building her global business around the environmental and human rights causes she campaigned so tirelessly for throughout her life, and eventually hanging up her CEO hat to become a full-time activist. Her classic: *Business as Unusual*.

ELEANOR ROOSEVELT • 1884–1962 • the "First Lady to the World"

The US's longest-serving first lady used the White House as her home base for advocacy and outreach from the Great Depression through WWII. A beloved humanitarian and founding UN diplomat, she's one of the most quoted women in history . . . and there's plenty of material to choose from between her 27 books, 580 articles, and 8,000+ columns. Dig into her mountain of content online at George Washington University's Eleanor Roosevelt Papers Project or look up one of our favorite titles—*You Learn by Living*.

SARAH ROSANEL • born 1985 • the doctor who answered the call for "all hands on deck"

Sarah had just started a cardiovascular fellowship at the Brooklyn hospital where she had completed her residency in internal medicine when the coronavirus pandemic hit New York. The Morocco-born, Paris-raised mother of three young children swiftly volunteered as an attending physician in a COVID-19 ward to see the city through the peak of the crisis. In her own words: her editorial for the American College of Cardiology, "Lessons Learned from COVID-19: We are All in it Together."

AMY KROUSE ROSENTHAL • 1965–2017 • the prolific author with a legacy

Amy inked more than 40 children's books along with a memoir, films, and a host of other creative ventures. But it's her column "You May Want to Marry My Husband" that you might want to find. Published just 10 days before she passed away from ovarian cancer, it's a tender love story that'll tug at your heartstrings. To add to a kid's bookshelf (no matter what age): *I Wish You More*. To visit: The giant yellow umbrella public art installation in Lincoln Park, Chicago (commissioned by the late author's husband).

SHARON SALZBERG • born 1952 • the insight & loving-kindness guide
After finding healing and a calling in Buddhist meditation, this spiritual leader has played a vital role in making the ancient practice speak to 21st-century life. Besides cofounding the nonprofit Insight Meditation Society and leading retreats, Sharon has authored 11 books—from *Real Happiness* to *Real Change* and hosts her own mindfulness podcast, *The Metta Hour*.

KENDRA SCOTT • born 1974 • the gem of a jewelry designer
Kendra started selling homemade jewelry to Austin, Texas, boutiques. She now has 100 of her own around the world. From her very first business venture—designing hats for chemo patients that would fund cancer research—she's always made social responsibility a pillar of her business plans. The same goes for her eponymous brand, which gives back to causes dear to the designer's heart: women's empowerment, education, and investing in up-and-comers. To hone those startup skills, check out: the University of Texas's Kendra Scott Women's Entrepreneurial Leadership Institute.

LILLY SINGH • born 1988 • the first woman of color to host a late-night show
Canadian-born Lilly was determined to be more than a Bollywood background dancer. The aspiring comedian decided to take her career into her own hands with quirky self-made sketch videos that went viral. The top YouTuber has retired her "IISuperwomanII" pseudonym for now to step out as the only lady of late-night network TV, but you can still binge-watch vids on her YouTube channel or read her tips on tenacity in *How to Be a Bawse*.

ELLEN JOHNSON SIRLEAF • born 1938 • the first female president of Liberia
This influential economist was forced to leave Liberia after she was repeatedly imprisoned for criticizing the country's military government while serving as a finance minister. She returned from exile to run for office, becoming Africa's first female elected head of state in 2006. During her 12-year tenure, she won a Nobel Peace Prize for furthering women's rights. In her own words: *This Child Will Be Great*.

SONIA SOTOMAYOR • born 1954 • the first Latina US Supreme Court justice
Sonia's early challenges—poverty, childhood diabetes, being raised by a single mom—inspired her passion for public service. From her days as a student civil rights activist to her first gig as a New York assistant district attorney to her tenure as the third woman to serve on the nation's top bench, Sonia has maintained a calm determination to ensure the law serves everyone. In her own words: *My Beloved World*. Also . . . *Just Ask!* to help kids accept and value their differences.

NICOLETTA SPAGNOLI • born 1955 • the innovative inheritor of a chic & sweet dynasty
This lauded Italian exec heads the stylish and delectable brands her great grandmother

built: the Luisa Spagnoli fashion line and Baci Perugina chocolates. Since taking over the companies as managing director in 1980, she's continued to put youthful, modern twists on their enduring traditions of quality and elegance. To enjoy: A Baci kiss.

MARTHA STEWART • born 1941 • the taste-making diva of domesticity
A former model and stockbroker turned caterer, Martha would become the US's first self-made female billionaire by building an iconic lifestyle brand out of her own Connecticut farmhouse. The media personality's reputation for scrupulous perfection took a tumble after a 2004 conviction linked to a stock sale. Since then, she's come back with the same zeal and flare, plus a few fabulous surprises, like her culinary collaborations with rapper Snoop Dogg. The book that made her a household name: *Entertaining*. Her recipes for entrepreneurship: *The Martha Rules*.

NICOLE STOTT • born 1962 • the self-proclaimed "artist, astronaut, earthling"
Nicole's adventures have seen her flying through space on two missions spanning 104 days and diving into the deepest depths of our oceans. The longtime NASA engineer can also boast painting the very first watercolor in space, which is on loan to the Smithsonian Institution's National Air and Space Museum in Washington, DC. Having taken in the splendors of Earth from many vantages, she's helping others discover the beauty of our planet via her foundation. To explore: the Space For Art website.

MERYL STREEP • born 1949 • the quintessential leading lady
Meryl—reverentially referred to as "The Streep" among acting students—is undisputed Tinseltown royalty. Her three Academy Awards and record for the most acting noms (21!) are testaments to her ability to absolutely nail real-life characters and her incredible versatility . . . as comfortable fronting madcap musicals and comedies as she is in gripping dramas. Though she's never been a fan of red-carpet glamour, it's a price she's willing to pay for the privilege of inhabiting and understanding the lives of others. To watch: her 2010 commencement address at Barnard College.

PAT SUMMITT • 1952–2016 • the star athlete & coaching legend
Growing up on a Tennessee farm, Pat went to a high school that didn't even have a girls' basketball team but ended up becoming one of the giants of the sport. She left the college game as the NCAA's winningest coach with eight championship titles to her name. Forced to retire due to early-onset Alzheimer's, Pat spent her final years rallying a team to help find a cure. Her classic: *Reach for the Summitt*, a how-to for leaders of all stripes.

MOTHER TERESA • 1910–1997 • the Nobel laureate canonized as a saint
This devout Macedonian nun felt called to religious service by the age of 12 and took vows at 21. While teaching in a Kolkata, India, Catholic school, she felt another calling—to go minister to "the unwanted, the unloved, the uncared for." She founded her own order,

the Missionaries of Charity, which gave rise to 610 foundations in 123 countries devoted to caring for the world's poor and sick. In her own words: *No Greater Love.*

GRETA THUNBERG • born 2003 • the climate change crusader

At age 15, Greta launched a personal protest. The Swedish student's decision not to go to school until governments took serious action on the climate crisis made headlines and set off a worldwide youth movement. *Time's* 2019 Person of the Year, Greta credits her Asperger's syndrome with giving her the singular focus necessary to endure trolls and speak so frankly, whether at mass rallies or on Capitol Hill. In her own words: *No One Is Too Small to Make a Difference.*

ABBY WAMBACH • born 1980 • the soccer superstar

The youngest of seven children, Abby was raised in a sports-loving family that inspired a love of healthy competition. Her sheer physicality and all-in team play have made her a clinch goal scorer. She's helped the US net the title in two Olympic Games and two FIFA World Cup championships that raised the profile of the women's game. The Hall of Famer is candid about her stumbles along the way and the importance of surrounding yourself with life's teammates who'll assist you in any situation. To watch: her 2017 commencement address at Barnard College, where she urges graduating seniors to not be like Little Red Riding Hood, but rather to be like the Wolf. And, find your own wolf pack.

VERA WANG • born 1949 • the wedding gown revolutionary

Once a figure skater hungry for a spot on the podium, Vera turned to fashion after her Olympic hopes were dashed. At age 23, she became *Vogue's* youngest ever senior editor. In her 40s, her own frustrating search for the right wedding dress saw her become a cutting-edge designer herself. Now one of the best-known names in the industry, the woman who brought bridal into the world of high fashion has translated her signature style into an accessible lifestyle brand. To read: "Life's Work," Vera's wide-ranging 2019 interview with *Harvard Business Review.*

EMMA WATSON • born 1990 • the actor-activist

This British actor was learning the ropes at a performing arts school when she was singled out to play a starring role in one of the most successful film franchises of all time. But Emma's career as a headliner didn't stop at Harry Potter's brainy BFF. She's gone from model to modern role model, taking time out from her acting schedule to study gender theory, lead empowering book groups, and engage millennials in much-needed conversations as a goodwill ambassador with UN Women. To follow: @oursharedshelf.

FRANCES WILLARD • 1839–1898 • the world-famous reformer

Frances was an accomplished educator who worked her way up from teacher in a one-room schoolhouse to president of a women's college before leaving academia to become a hugely influential lobbyist. As a founding member and longtime president of the Woman's Christian Temperance Union, Frances made it the largest women's organization of the 19th century and a political force to be reckoned with. Though she's best known for promoting a ban on alcohol, she effectively championed women's suffrage, labor rights, and prison reform. To visit, in person or virtually: National Statuary Hall in the US Capitol, Washington, DC (Frances was the first woman to have a statue among the greats in this grand hall).

JODY WILLIAMS • born 1950 • the broker of the Mine Ban Treaty
As an international aid worker in war-torn El Salvador, Jody had the grim job of providing artificial limbs to children who lad lost arms and legs to land mines. When the opportunity arose to coordinate an international coalition to ban the concealed explosive devices and deal with the 100 million still buried around the world, she took it. Her efforts led to a historic treaty ratified by 130 countries (and counting) and earned her a Nobel Peace Prize. In her own words: *My Name Is Jody Williams*. To look up: the site of her latest project, Nobel Women's Initiative.

SERENA WILLIAMS • born 1981 • the tennis GOAT
A tennis pro for more than two decades, this powerhouse with a 128-mph serve is the winningest player of the Open Era, with 23 Grand Slam titles (not to mention 16 doubles titles and 4 Olympic golds) to her name. Besides being the oldest woman to rank #1 and the world's highest-earning female athlete, she's an active philanthropist with a serious side hustle as an inclusive fashion designer whose mantra is #BeSeenBeHeard.

REESE WITHERSPOON • born 1976 • the unapologetically ambitious actor
Long billed as Hollywood's bubbly "girl next door," this Oscar-winning actor has emerged as an outspoken mover and shaker. An entrepreneur, producer, and tastemaker with her own clothing line and book club, Reese is using her resources and influence to spotlight stories that might otherwise go unseen. Along the way, she's proving that investing in women-driven narratives yields financial and social returns. In her own words (inspired by her Southern upbringing): *Whiskey in a Teacup*.

MALALA YOUSAFZAI • born 1997 • the youngest Nobel laureate
When a Taliban gunman tried to assassinate the 15-year-old Malala on her way home from school, her voice for girls' right to learn only got stronger. The education activist with her own foundation became the global face of children's rights, leaving a wave of powerful youth activists in her wake. In her own words: *I Am Malala*. To follow: @MalalaFund. To watch: her "16th birthday speech" at the UN (the first after recovering from a gunshot to the head).

Gratefully.

Encouraging Women Across All Borders

a nonprofit launched by young women to support female undergraduates

Sparked by an intro from accomplished business exec Lisa Mascolo, who's among Quotabelle's earliest champions and investors, we debuted a six-week Bravely digital publishing internship with 19 college students from seven universities spanning five countries. As the implications of the global coronavirus pandemic were unfolding, these young women worked in teams to research five remarkable women featured in Quotabelle's book *Bravely* and this guided journal. The interns collaborated virtually, conducting research and delivering presentations via Zoom, all while their own college studies and day-to-day lives were upended. We're inspired by the talent, tenacity, and creativity of these up-and-coming leaders. And we're beyond grateful.

Thanks to their efforts, you can discover the stories and sourced quotations of the following greats on Quotabelle.com: Nobel laureate Jody Williams, game-changing model Halima Aden, rocket scientist turned Girl Scouts CEO Sylvia Acevedo, software engineering pioneer Margaret Hamilton, and algorithm innovator on the team that created the first image of a black hole Katie Bouman.

Encouraging Women Across All Borders (EWAAB)

CEO and cofounder: Kaitlin Gili

Cofounder: Dominika Ďurovčíková

Program coordinator & internship director: Sam Collins

California Institute of Technology • California, USA

Interns: Alexandra Haraszti • Arielle Tycko • Abigail Jiang • Juliette Koval

Primary mentor: Sam Davis

Secondary mentor: Professor Xie Chen

College of William & Mary • Virginia, USA

Intern: Ella Schotz

Primary mentor: Hana Warner

Secondary mentor: Dr. Irina Novikova

Comenius University • Bratislava, Slovakia

Interns: Laura Galajdová • Flora Sedlarova

Primary mentor: Laura Adamkovičová

Secondary mentor: Monika Čičová

KU Leuven • Leuven, Belgium

Interns: Nalan Yaylaci • Laetitia Fokou • Margot Delaet • Sriyaa Srinivasan

Primary mentor: Uliana Durbak

Secondary mentor: Dr. Vero Vanden Abeele

Stevens Institute of Technology • New Jersey, USA

Interns: Amira Saied • Pamela Karasmilova • Sanjana Madhu • Christine Huang

Primary mentor: Kaitlin Gili

Secondary mentor: Hoveida Nobakht

University of Melbourne • Melbourne, Australia

Interns: Chanel le Roux • Malaila Safdar • Megnot Tesfaye Seyoum

Primary mentor: Celia Dowling

Secondary mentor: Dr. Linden Ashcroft

University of Oxford • Oxford, England

Intern: Gabrielle Rostand

Primary mentor: Dominika Ďurovčíková

Secondary mentor: Professor Adrianne Slyz

RP Studio & Running Press (Hachette Book Group)
We adore collaborating with this smart and immensely
creative publishing team
• Shannon Fabricant • Jenna McBride • Ashley Benning •
• Alina O'Donnell • Kristin Kiser •

InkWell Management
Our literary agents are champions and coaxers extraordinaire
• Alexis Hurley • Kim Witherspoon •

Our Quotabelle community
We remain ever appreciative of our families & friends, investors
& advisers, Quotabelle's early thinkers & builders, plus our
growing community of quote & story lovers whose support remains
central to helping us continue the work toward achieving our
own audacious dream.

About us

PAULINE WEGER
SOCIAL ENTREPRENEUR • INVENTOR • AUTHOR • CITESEER

Pauline stepped away from her corporate career to launch Quotabelle, a conscious company—including a patented platform—built on a vision of creatively introducing more female role models to the world. Mom to two daughters (a millennial and a Gen Z), she and her husband recently moved to the Pioneer Valley in western Massachusetts.

ALICIA WILLIAMSON, PHD
CHIEF EDITOR • RESEARCHER • AUTHOR • CITESEER

Alicia is a wayfaring academic who loves using her keystrokes for good. This former prof turned chief editor is a research aficionado with a passion for digging in archives, especially to unearth hidden ideas and stories from remarkable women & girls. A Minnesota native, Alicia, her husband, and two daughters (a toddler and an infant) are settling into their new home in North East England.

We discover the ideas and stories of real women and girls.
And make them shareable.

To spark innovation. To create connections. To bring balance to the world.

Our books, programs, and products-for-good inspire everyday living—from offices to classrooms, family rooms to kid's rooms, studios to sports fields, in print and online.

DISCOVER HER STORY
• www.quotabelle.com •
on Instagram, Facebook and Twitter @quotabelle

RP Studio™
Hachette Book Group
1290 Avenue of the Americas, New York, NY 10104
www.runningpress.com
@Running_Press

Printed in Singapore

First Edition: March 2021

Published by RP Studio, an imprint of Perseus Books, LLC, a subsidiary of Hachette Book Group, Inc. The RP Studio name and logo is a trademark of the Hachette Book Group.

The publisher is not responsible for websites (or their content) that are not owned by the publisher.

Design by Jenna McBride.
Patterns copyright © Getty Photos

ISBN: 978-0-7624-7152-2

1010

10 9 8 7 6 5 4 3 2 1

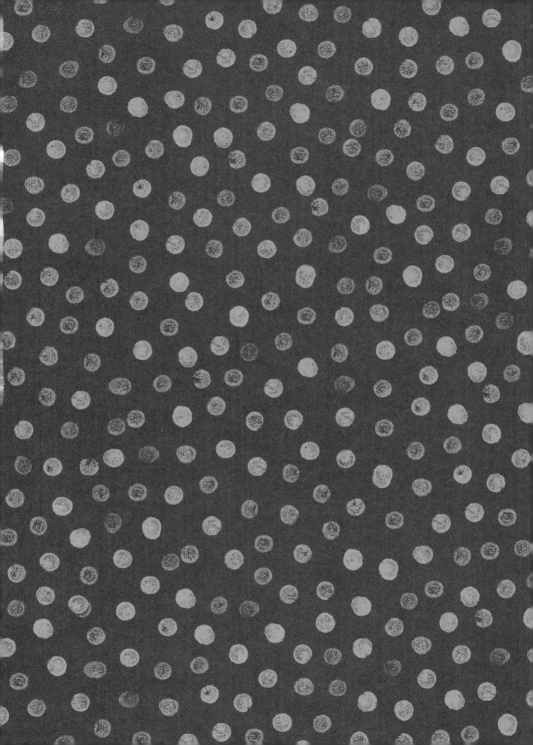